MANEUVERS

CHRISTOPHER DEWEESE

BLUE HOUR PRESS

2011

.

Blue Hour Press • 1526 Kentucky St • Lawrence KS 66044
www.bluehourpress.com • editor@bluehourpress.com

ISBN 978-1-257-98266-0

ACKNOWLEDGEMENTS

I would like to thank the editors of the following journals in which these poems first appeared, sometimes in slightly different forms: *Bateau, Cannibal, Invisible Ear, notnostrums.com, Phoebe, Pool, Skein, SIR!,* and *Zoland Poetry Annual.*

**WINTER IS COLD, PROTECTORS SCARCE,
"ROMANCE" IS NOT IN COMMAND.**

CARL MARTIN

INTERNING FOR GHOSTS

I have no war to talk myself into,
my hands lost in the sentiment
of cannon-fire
without the amputations
that surely exist
within a cannonball's conception of the future.
Even now, behind the ropes
of this museum
my heart has carved uncertainly,
bayonets in place of placards
and you a regiment
I guide nightly, all of you
smuggled like radio signals
where my teeth have been,
I have no enemies.
Lost with only weather for a hero,
the sky knows me well.
Divination seems possible
when tree branches are backlit.
An epigraph the sun crochets.
A settler's nasty churn.
A curse to blanket us with.

THE FRENCHMAN

No flag to plant you with,
I turn to this tongue,
this strange helpful child I keep.
Clouds brother themselves above us
as if your men
had trapped the spirits,
the enormous wigs
we scratch for guidance
as the shipwrecked might
paw thin coins,
their Queen's face.
We sit cross-legged.
This proves many things:
that we aren't afraid
for our children,
that we are truly men.
Your women must be hidden far away.
I imagine them
carving scrimshaw
from the frozen rivers,
swans from the frozen lakes.
I imagine them constantly,
a horizon into my lungs.
When I finally dream,
I will dream these furs covering me
are wigs of real hair,
and I will wake
like a bog painted over.

When we smoke,
something between us leavens.
The swan in your eyes
moves me,
but my heart is so far away
it might as well be thunder,
might have just invented postcards.
I write this treaty in the snow.
Now I write it in giant flames.

12 ANTIQUE POSTCARD

I'm going back
to the atheist suburbs of my life,
where there is no you
and the wars seem more honest,
tattoos of garlic or asparagus
covering teenage arms,
the lost flags of community agriculture.
Outside, the sky builds a library
from the imaginary hours
when farming was just for fun.
Birds spangle the harvest
and bears mentor wild men,
smudging domestic pollen
like slam-dancing
through a cornucopia.
You can hear brambles
scratching thin scars against the wind.
If you close your eyes,
you can see Native Americans.

THE SOLDIER

The orders were straightforward:
catapult the traitor
into the constellation we were building,
a giant moat above us.
The General knew this was unpopular.
"Remember: the enemy
tried to kill your children," he said.
"We believe they're fifty percent sorcerer
with a little alligator."
I tried to imagine their faces
like witchy handbags,
but I had a hard time combining things.
"How much help will you need
when your daughter is tied to a windmill?"
the general screamed.
It sounded rhetorical
so the fifth platoon went to sleep again,
dreaming the headlines around us
as the trebuchet readied itself
like a tethered scorpion.
My blood felt the geography
of the prisoner's skin
when I tucked him in upon his boulder.

WAX MESSAGE

Change your face
when you miss me being useless.
Use the finger language of divers
to sign your own name.
The alphabet of flag
mistakes patriotism for distress.
When heated,
white vinegar turns red.
Throw a graph in the garbage
when you see me.
Cut a graph from your beard.
I'll be pencil dust,
waiting for indentations.
You'll be the wind that betrays us.

THE BEST MAN

"I am the best man," I said.
"Where do I go?"
The tree didn't say anything.
It looked magical.
It looked studious and natural,
the first tree at the edge of the forest.
I poured a little Jack Daniels
down its moss.
I poured some coke in a circle.
A few leaves fell off
the well-proportioned branches,
revealing an owl.
I said "Now you're getting wild."
I said "What's your friend's name?"
I was in an open relationship.
I started telling jokes.
I looked amazing
in my camouflage tuxedo.

CONCESSION SPEECH

Outside this platform,
ice-sculptures of swans melt,
leaving dollar signs,
and all you men
are bed-less tonight,
backs slightly broken
past the highway's tooth-less humming
and my mistakes:
the foghorns I mounted
on riverbanks devoid of freight or fog,
the municipal fires
I let hoboes register.
Cue the sob stories
about the dead and simple guys
who can't vote
because they think we're ghosts
or whatever.
As we roll up the jungle
the streamers and confetti
would have been,
I can almost hear
the loud song.
Inside me, there is all this dust
I want to have a reason for.

THE PILGRIM

Lost, I've been haunting
the national breezeway,
but I am no bird.
The Lord I've searched for
founds an expert fraternity
between dawn and rehab
when I doubt myself,
unscrewing my teeth
and jangling them in his pockets.
Angels confuse me for castanets.
Now I'm underground.
Down here, even pointy hats
can't distract the flames.
Help: I'm melting into fossils!

18   THE TERRIFIED PEOPLE

I found the terrified people
clutching twigs and branches.
In a clearing of their own devising,
they were trying to settle down.
Around them,
the clearing was full of loudspeakers
and some animals.
The wind felt diagonal,
banging its harsh song
against the thatches.
A skinless world
vibrated against our own,
like a drum only softer.
Over the carnal hillside,
troop movements made sense again.
I radioed my lieutenant,
yowling plainly
into the forest.
It was time to bring in the darkness.

STAGECOACH

Chad is untouchable.
Martin is Swedish.
Clad in these and other signifiers,
our heroes dismount at the village.
That I would have once been there
to sup their horses water
is a minor exposition,
a military tattoo
beat upon the parchment wind.
Asleep in the future's prequel,
ghosts waltz under each spur's jangle
like stage directions
and I am one of them,
a single pirouette
spun again and again.
Motion built this franchise,
a cardboard western
burning its own streets
to smoke out villains.
The saloon is still open,
serving whiskey at room temperature
like tiny flames
to keep nasty gasps lit.
The rest of Wyoming is abandoned:
it's just me and Willie Nelson,
and that's the way I like it.

THE SPHINX

Ordained by my laziness
to sleep through the entire day
it takes to reach the Sphinx,
I dreamt it wore your face.
When I finally woke,
chambermaids were throwing rocks
all over my shadow.
I freaked out
and thought about calling you,
but the phone was full of sand.
I could only hear insects.
All and all, it felt beautiful,
like when we slept
in the infinite motels of America
and never opened their bibles.

COMMAND COMMAND

Corporals dream, we dream
in residential logistics:
the cost of silver uniforms,
a stipend for the hobo,
the precise width of each flagpole.
We weed this neighborhood
of "To Whom It May Concern"
in favor of morale-building aliases
like Golden Bag or Sex Hawk.
If our dreams lack weather,
they must be federally mandated.
They must be stored somewhere,
possibly as murals
or in the evidence time-capsules sequester,
some for posterity
and some for confession.
The problem with memories
is when we zoom in
and stop the tape right here,
we realize there is only one house
one tree and one car
repeating like a preview
for the most boring dream ever.
Immaculate, geometric blocks
revise our histories
into an endless, socialist landscape:
something inside us
has turned, an emoticon

22   whose wink has been replaced
by bolts and nuts.
To be honest, it feels great.
Without a setting, only plot remains.
If there is no plot,
we'll just keep on smoking cigarillos
and sticking pins into the big table.

OH TRICILLIAN

Oh Tricillian,
the shadows are all wrong!
And I don't believe you're guilty,
but your name is on the tree,
and the tree is like a gun
smoking through the third act
in that it killed your mistress
in front of everyone.
Reading the pathologist's report in bed
the evidence speaks to me,
a quiet island where ghosts get flattened.
Exhibit A: we all have lungs.
We share the air,
and the light slowly kills us.
"All trails are incidental to begin with,"
said the inspector,
his voice running gloves
across the baseboards
as men dusted pheasants
from our small, domestic forest.
The sherry came late and trembling
and you fainted, Tricillian,
leaving the rest of us
shaking in the rotunda
with nothing proper to eat
but biscuits and cold mutton.

POCKET MAP

Lost in a so-so garden,
I couldn't see to haunt anything.
Darkness dug swamps
between the suburbs
and my position,
a cold wind taking shadows
for strange machines.
Parallel to my flesh,
a scarecrow lifted flags.
Tatters mapped the airspace.
It seemed to be midnight
or else it was raining hard
and I was translucent.
I tried to move but I couldn't.
A failed crop of dried-up poppies
crackled underfoot
like a welcome mat.
Where was the farmer
who planted his fields in buckshot
to sleep more easily?
Where was the obituary
my pockets were empty for,
the answering machine
where your voice slept
singing tin-pan standards?

JUST THE FACTS

There is no equation more beautiful
than X = X.
No emoticon more honest than 0.
We pressed our thumbs
over solar-powered calculators.
The digits faded
into rabbits.
Time capsules were a crop.
Clouds were the future.
Everything we did,
we did in real time.
We shot more meat than we could carry.
We tried to ford the river.
The buffalo cried.

26 THE DESERTERS

Meet me at the company store.
Bring your government bag,
your dreams of weather.
Casual, we'll thresh percentages,
gently sequester the sea
behind the square tents
and evening locusts.
We'll find a common leisure
inside the wilderness,
uniforms fading around us
like taxable silhouettes,
a corporate wilderness.
When we're sleeping,
this makes sense.
All year, we've been drilling
to prepare for winter,
asleep for days
and then for weeks
like understudies
to a real, living mother.

ABOUT THE AUTHOR

Christopher DeWeese lives in Northampton, Massachusetts. His first book, *The Black Forest*, will be published by Octopus Books in 2012. His poems have appeared in *Boston Review*, *Fence*, and *Tin House*.

www.ingramcontent.com/pod-product-compliance
Lightning Source LLC
Chambersburg PA
CBHW022351040426
42449CB00006B/830